Dear You,

Dear You,

www.softasbones.com
Instagram: @softasbones
Twitter: @softasbones
Patreon: softasbones

It's all a part of the journey.

INCINERATE

It starts as a small crack—
just a hairline incision
at the top of my cranium.

Incrementally,
it's as if a hand
is placed on both sides,
pulling the skin
amalgamating
my bones—

I can hear the tear
emerging from the separation
of flesh and flesh—
the licking and smacking
of a tongue to its roof—

Until the ripping exceeds
my ear drums,
past the shoulders,
through the heart,
down the pelvis,
until two things remain:

The side who is me,
and the side incinerated
by you.

THE LAND OF EVERLASTING SMILES

Everyone is searching for it—
the rarest thing of all:

the lasting smiles.

Perhaps they walk off the faces
of the humans underneath,
because their minds are too much darkness
to ever stay, for too long—
so they decide it's time to go;
kissing, licking, and smacking their way,
to the land of
everlasting smiles.

THE CRESCENT MOON

I wore a smile
the way people
wear an accessory—

at the end
of the day
I would take it off,

hang it up,
watch my reflection
shift from a perception

into
a horizontal
flip sided
moon.

TRUST ISSUES

You never understood
why the accusations would start,
but you always noticed
when my eyes shifted
from the girl you loved,
into the girl
you didn't recognize.

CHILDHOOD

When I was little,
   I loved my father.
He was so big and strong.
   I felt protected,
because I knew
no one could get through him—
   but it was sad
because I never knew
the one I needed protection from,
   was him.

FAMILIARITY

Danger doesn't hide
      in darkness.
It sits in the open,
staring you in the eyes—
        watching and waiting,
        methodically constraining.
It tackles you in the form
      of familiarity.
Don't "watch your back,"

look straight ahead.

THE CLOSE ONES

They say only the people you love can hurt you,
I wish I didn't know that to be true.

THE PEBBLE

Perhaps i'm simply
too complicated,
too mosaic,
too much lightning—
I'm the little pebble
that's jagged and rough—
but I promise
when you find the right spot
you've never felt anything
as soft as me.

LONELY

You can call me the tumbleweed—
for the wind is my only friend,
rolling down rocky roads,
on the pursuit of a new bend.

BEAUTIFUL

Laying naked, nothing on
besides my pink laced panties.
"You're beautiful."
       How can you tell?
Have you glimpsed beneath my smile—
soft squishy skin coating bones,
as candle wax melts
along the holder:
equally as perishable,
my clockwork flame—
carefully, creepily, undoubtedly,
       melting away my skin,
searing away seduction,
       charcoal flesh.

Tell me something:
when you're staring into a pile of my bones,
       what will you miss?
black hair falling past big brown eyes,
olive skin draped over long lickable legs—
diving between thighs,
unlocking oceans—
craving tiny explosive embers
lacing my vein rivers,
       a meadow of dreams.

Did you notice it?
Perhaps your flesh only noticed mine,
ignorant to the demons which fuelled it—
Is it possible to call something beautiful
      if you've never really seen it?
you watched me,
sunshine chasing moon—
never really feeling me,
never really noticing—
      only tasting,
      taking me,
until the last of our days
when you looked—

moonlit draped skin
shredded into ashes of flesh
      picking up
      floating away
into
p i x e l a t e d
memories

was she beautiful?

THE OLD FORGOTTEN SOCK

I was an old forgotten sock
         t u m b l e d
underneath the bed—
There, I sat.
But it was more of a heap—
There, I heaped.
Amalgamated with the carpet,
bristles bristling
against my flushed
pink cheek—

I wished it was snow,
something cold to numb
this painful heat—
this break was supposed to be clean
         and neat.

Dust had collected,
and after a little time had
         p a s s e d,
you came and had a look—
blew right on me,
sending away
         the dirt,
only to pick me up,
put me on your foot,
and walk
         all o v e r me.

SEEDLING

How can such a beautiful tree come
from such a terrible root?

The water that fed the seed
must've been laced with deceit—

I guess it's a good thing
the soil has been changed,

for I fear what this tree
might've became.

COCAINE COWBOY

I laid in your bed,
checking the clock—
w a i t i n g,
hearing every single tock.

"Wait here for me.
I'll be back in one hour,
and the night
will be ours."

But it had been two,
        now three,
and then at four,
I slipped into a snore.

Beep.Beep.Beep
6:45am
You were stumbling in,
while I was stumbling out.

You apologized,
with liquor on your bite,
and your nose
dripping white.

VIOLET

For a time,
my violet petals
were painted on—

the rain came
washing my pigment away—
revealing,

black petals wilted,
shaded from the sun.

DEPRESSION

I laid with each limb
stretched and fallen
far away from my body—

it was as if they were apart
of something else—

I was the candle wax
burning deep,
        s p r e a d i n g,
melting away—

and everything else
was afraid to touch me.

ANXIETY

I fell through the crack—
tumbled right down.
It was dark and black,
but I never felt the ground.

COLORFUL BOY

It's the way
you look from your eyes
but see through your heart—

painting me in colour,
       masking the greys,
blowing off my sadness,
and sending it far away.

THE PODIUM

I was so misled by loved ones,
my life was manipulated without knowledge.

I was so misled by confusion,
my life evolved into a big ball of frustration.

I was so misled by reality,
my life was full of unending questions—

nobody gets it, nobody knows.

TRAUMA BOND

The burnt in me
saw the atrophy in you—
and together we strolled
confessing all our sins.

A COLORFUL DECEIT

How can it be so?
that a love this deep—
one that only grows,
can make me feel cold
       and helplessly
alone.

A SHADOW

Slow belly creep
grasps heart,
seizes lungs,
grips limbs,
         infects brain—

dark thoughts
         lacing veins,
from the shadow
you keep me in—

the longer i'm hidden,
the worse it becomes.

UN-AFFAIR

The confusion in you
is the unraveling in me.

INADVERTENT PARAMOUR

How did it taste when you licked my toes
and traced it down my calves,
my thighs, my lips—
  Was it cinnamon sweet?

How did it feel when you ran your hands
up my skirt, grabbing my panties,
pulling them down—
  Was it barbie soft?

What did you think when you talked of babies,
promising rings, love forever, always magic,
old and grey—
  Did you feel remorse?

Was it happiness when you put me
on my knees, pulled down your pants, told me to choke,
swallow, daddy's little whore—
  Did you love it when I asked for more?

How did you do it when you would go home,
look her in the eyes, kiss her, love her,
fuck her—
  Did you think of me when you were between her?

What was the logic when you listened to my pain,
dad abusing daughter, learning to love, to trust,
seizing my issues—
  Was it your enchanting game?

How could come home to me from her,
hop on top of me, kiss me, bite me,
fuck me—
        Did you not feel filthy?
I feel filthy.

You took my love, trust, fears
and dirtied them with lies—

You took everything I told you, all my pain,
laughed at it while you fucked her,
laughed at me when you slid
your filthy cock inside me—
        Was my sadness an echo
        when your dick thrusted inside her?

When you wished I was your son's mother,
you relegated her to nothing—
only a mother, worthless, overthinker,
        "You RUIN everything."

How could you say that to her?

You made us both feel worthless,
when really you were the worthless one,
all along.

THE FOG

I took off the rose petals from my eyes
and finally seen you for what you are.

SOILED

You took something so beautiful
and dirtied it with your lies.

TOO OFTEN

Two little words
are your favourite ones to utter—
       spoken often
by the most selfish of all:

"I'm sorry."

REFLECTION

Did you ever stop to think,
what am I doing here?
What are my actions
         my words
doing to this beautiful,
yet fragile
and complicated soul?

But who can pause
         and reflect
how they affect another,
when they can't even pause
         to reflect
on how they affect
         themselves.

TAINTED

Two broken people
unveiled themselves,
gave themselves—
      o p e n e d,
uncovered.

Now, you hide me;
black veiled curtains—
      alone,
behind this velvet sheet.

Sometimes
you take a peek,
but it is brief—
and a reminder

i'm not yours,
and might never be.

BYE BYE

I want to know why—
why you had to make me cry.

I want to know why—
you were the one who chose to lie.

I want to know why—
all the memories we have,
have all turned to bad.

You used to be my father,
now I won't even bother.

PRECARIOUS

Happiness,
isn't it strange?

Here today,
        gone tomorrow.

A DELICACY

You came to me on that day
when my face was a rain-filled window.
       "I can fix this, I can make this better."

You hugged me,
kissed my forehead,
thinking you were becoming
the good guy in my story.

You believed it so well
that my body had no choice but to
      r e l i n q u i s h
under the conviction in your eyes.

When did you decide
to become another one
      of the bad ones?

Didn't you know
I was broken to begin with?

ONE EYE OPEN

And sometimes we should fear
the ones with great intentions,
because they have superpowers—

trouble is,
they don't always use them for good.

DANCING SMILES

That's the thing with the melancholy soul—
it just returns to its natural state,
once the intermittent smiles
have danced themselves
away.

CONVENIENT LIES

It was just so much easier that way;
I hate you,
              made me feel better
     than
            i l o v e y o u.

THE LONGEST NAP

I need someone
to wash away the world,
smash away the responsibilities,
that prevent me
from sleeping.

GAME OVER

Always on your time,
your rules,
your convenience—

this is a game
i just opted out of.

A COLLISION

You were like that—
           strong and steady.

I was weak,
you were gravity
           a tethering gaze—
everytime I floated away,

you were the earth,
and I was the asteroid.

THE BEAR

I walked into a backyard filled with broken stones and blocks of wood and that's where you sat—a broad back, muscles I traced into memories with fingertips. Your head didn't turn—you stared off into the distance as if you were also wherever that distance was. But your body was here, tense and cold, even though the sun was beating down on it. A slight turn of the head and a slight breath of "hi," was how you acknowledged my presence. I sat down next to you, dancing a toy bear along your leg in the hopes it would crack your demeanor. I put down the soapstone bear and sat down next to you—knowing you weren't ready to come back to this patch of grass with ants crawling all over it. I laid down next to you, feeling the warmth of the sun, playing over different scenarios inside my mind for how I could bring you back from that faraway place, right next to me. Time passed in this moment as if each minute were five, hyper-aware of every shift in your muscles. "Do you want to pretend to be an animal and I guess what it is?" "No." And so I laid again, knowing I would never leave you alone to deal with your demons.

You crave aloneness because it's how you keep yourself safe—it's how you've always kept yourself safe. I know that well. But further past your barricade of aloneness is you as a child, thankful for my presence refusing to leave you alone.

And so that's what I did, I ignored your feeble attempts to convince me why being around you won't be fun.

I laid next to you, showing that no dark part of you will push me away. I tried and tried to bring you back, creating a new excuse each time to get your mind back on the present, back right here, next to me. You didn't eat, so I concocted a plan. You refused me when I said let's have a barbeque, let's have fun. So I tried again—a new tactic. I got up from your sun glaring spot and went to the barbeque, "Does this thing work? I'm gonna go to the store and make some food." I knew your meat-perfecting barbeque soul would never let me cook on that thing by myself. So I gathered my things in the house, and sure enough you followed me in—you told me you'll come with me, and slowly, but surely, I could see the you that I know and love returning back from your journey. The darkness of your eyes faded away, and by the end of the night your eyes shone a bright green hazel as you laid down next to me.

"We're in dangerous water."

A RELIANCE

I lay on the mattress
incapable of moving
so you stood for me—

making pancakes,
and forcing a smile—
with syrup—
to my lips.

A MESS

I stood in the bedroom
staring into shards of brokenness—
and the only thing left to do
was grab a broom.

MY TOXIC LOVE

And that's just the way
we operated—
I could cry and yell
and you would
       yell louder,
       and cry softer—
but when we went too far
the other knew
       it was time
to forget themselves
and become exactly
what the other
needed.

PENDULUM

Why is it so impossible
to say goodbye—
and be able to mean it.

A LESSON LEARNED

You should never have to convince him
what you mean to him.

UNSEEN

Don't let the reasons to stay
blind you from the millions
of reasons to go.

MIRROR

It is not your responsibility
to hold up a mirror to his heart
when he is too afraid to face
what's inside himself.

BONE DEEP

You are the needle
piercing flesh—
swimming
in my veins
to the marrow,
leaving your mark
to the bone.

A DANGER

It's easy for them
to look at you
and wonder
        what the fuck
you're doing,

but they haven't felt
the shivers
down your spine
when he kisses
your shoulder—

they haven't felt
        the warmth
inside your heart
after a million
        cold nights—

they don't know
what it's like
to drink his tongue,
        having it lick
all the broken crevices
inside that
beautiful,
but shattered
soul.

WEATHERMAN

You are the calm—
you are the storm.

THE SABOTAGE

I could ask you
        why wasn't I enough,

but I want you to ask yourself—
        why didn't I deserve her?

A SENSE

You stared at me as if
I was the most beautiful,
precious thing in the world—

soaking up
each angle of my face,
        squeezing in
every ounce
        of my love,
because you could sense

I was gearing up
        to leave—
for good.

FLIPPANT TONGUES

Your words are big—
filled with lavender,
lilacs, and gold.

Too bad your words
have been the only
sweetness—

while your actions,
merely a colossal
disappointment.

DISARRAY

And the end
        was a star blazing
until it stretched out and
        s h a t t e r e d
its dust all over.

A BLUR

Maybe you're blind, vision blurred—
like Vaseline smeared on a mirror;

maybe you're too selfish, too conceited
because my love is a bird,
and you are my migration;

maybe you forgot what it's like
to live without my words of devotion,
there for you to gobble up
with every ounce of gluttony;

maybe my heart showers
no longer saturate you—
growing dry with your insatiable
need of me and her;

maybe I'm tired of wondering,
tired of emptying myself for you—
let her be your shower,
cause I'm not doing maybes anymore.

SEVERING

Broken glass,
shattered mess,
all wrong—
but sometimes
I still miss
the moments
that felt right.

THE COURT

Would you follow me
into the darkness—
let the stars be our light,
and dance with me
into the wee hours
                of the night.

PERCEPTION

You had a way of splattering
my body with stars,
but everyone only saw the daylight—

I looked different at night.

HARD LESSON

The glimpses you gave me
of what you could be—
    how sweet,
    how loving,
was not worth
    the deception,
    the lies,
the irrevocable
feelings of
pain.

A CHERRY BLOSSOM TREE—

I was the petals,
you were the branch;
you shook in the wind,
and I fell to the ground.

HOME TIME

I don't know how to live without you,
but it is painful to know you.

SHARP FINGERS

Somewhere Stewart cooks
       and Hubert smacks
and I heard the rainbow
       is over somewhere,
like Marjory.

Oh fancyland,
       enough.

Bowrain dust where
       some shine sun,
blue are skies.
       Heavens blue,
       fish blue,
Baxter and Jeremy—
       blue too.

The red water comes out,
       I like it.

FLEETING

Dear little girls
with blades
to your flesh:
        put it down,
this is only temporary—
I promise.

A MEMORY

Spiralled staircase—
          small body;
a glimpse into a bedroom.

Pink precious bedsheets
          lacking innocence,
poignant sins—

A large hand
shutting the door—
          only a glimpse

of her pink stained eyes,
while I spiralled,
with the staircase.

INHERENT FEAR

I walk home late at night
and as a woman,
I make myself small—
       clinging
to the shadows.

A car drives
slowly my way
       and I retreat
to the bushes.

Someone walks
toward me
and I cross the street.

When I leave
the well-lit sidewalk
inching closer to my home,
       I sprint full-tilt
until I close the door
behind me—
       heart racing;

thankful that
for another night,
I managed to stay
       anonymous.

WHAT I'VE ALWAYS KNOWN

You were chaos,
and that's exactly why
I felt right at home with you.

NO MORE

Being around you
is as if my insides
shrink into a ball—

leaving my skin
as a woven
shell of me—

that's how I knew
it was time to go.

THE LAPPING

Cold and crashing,
       you came raging
until your waters grasped,
pulling me in—

softly licking
       with a silly smile,
tonguing my wounds,
sealing me in—

toppling below,
       I threw myself
until you dove deep,
pulling me out—

you were the eb,
and I was the flow.

MISFIT

Different places,
I don't belong,
and all the faces,
each all wrong—

the grass beneath,
here I sit,
the only place
I seem to fit.

CUMULONIMBUS

I am summer's breeze
and you're the calm of heat—

together we build storms,
raw and uncontrolled—

until I tire of lightning,
you release the thunder—
and together we let it rain,
          w a s h i n g a w a y
broken hampers
and smashed candle glass—

come kiss me one last time,
and promise it's the last,
just as the last.

SORROW MORROW

Lost puddles drip,
        ooze
until they overflow
and have no choice
but to f a l l
away from the threshold—
        splat.

A trail of memories
revert backwards
until we find the beginning—
        echo.

No longer there
and all has drained out
until the whole
is barricaded walls—
        hollow.

The familiar vacancy
that never leaves my side—
my dear friend,
        Melancholy.

UNDERNEATH THE
WAVE

Static lines,
drawing out—
chasing horizons.

Folding up,
falling over—
submerging beneath.

Melancholic laughter,
piercing seagulls—
horizontal crescent moons.

There's honey melting
from the sky.

THE CALCULATOR

Salt dripping,
        silk sheets,
"I love you,"
false sweets.

INTRINSIC DESTRUCTION

Standing at the window,
everything enflamed—
buildings lit,
smoke's spit.

The world ached,
but we stood
in our desolate room,
staring at everything
that meant something.

We watched it burn,
grabbed each other's hand,
and jumped.

BORDERLINE

You fill my heart with hatred
with every passing day
of your I don't knows.

THE HUNTER

Be a wolf with me—
zip up the fuzzy costume
and leave the traces
of our humanity behind.

Come stalk with me
in the shadows and trees,
where we'll catch bunnies
          and then release
before hunting them again—

look into their eyes,
see the pleading,
the helplessness—

maybe then you'll understand
          the weight
of your predatory ways.

MANIPULATE

The gravity of you
pulls at my moon—

love of a woman
with daddy issues—

is sometimes
easily abused.

THE TORCH

You filled my nights
with anxiety gaslights,

attempting to drive me
into your psyche—

I hope one day
you learn what love is.

OUR GREAT PERIL

The complications in me,
love the complications in you.

THE SWITCH

Sometimes you can spend years with another person and slowly over time a natural distance occurs—even though you are side by side your souls are moving further and further apart.

Other times something opposing happens. You can spend so much time with another person and your soul loves being next to theirs—maybe a little too much, to the point of toxicity. You know you have to let go—to force the distance, and yet it's the hardest thing you've ever had to do.

Why is it that sometimes distance occurs even though it's not what you want, and then other times when all you want is to feel that freedom, feel that sense of disconnect, feel anything other than that stupid sense of joy when you're with them—why does the distance not come when you want it?

I wish I could flip a switch inside my heart rendering my care nonexistent, but sadly I am not a work of fiction. I am not a character in a novel or sci-fi, fantasy book where I could write up my own button and place it inside my brain and then when my emotions are too high, too unbearable, too unstable, I could look within my fictitious mind and turn it all off.

The saddest part of it all is that I'm not even certain my fictitious self would be strong enough to turn that switch off—I still envy fictitious me because she at least has the choice to turn it off.

I'm just stuck with my feelings and the battleground inside my mind that fights each day to shut you off.

Why can't I shut you off?

A TWIN FLAME

I was quiet and alert—
absorbing every word,
             c a r e s s i n g
everything that hurt.

I knew the feeling
             of drowning,
by my surroundings—

so there I sat,
with a confused man,
falling in love
with his sad.

THE PULL

Insane and impractical—
I can't help myself,
because you
          are fucking magical.

THE OSCAR

You blame your mind
for actions of your body,
but it was your heart that was acting—
       not your brain.

ONYX

Some days you were the hardest
thing to break through—
with eyes like obsidian.

Other days your smile cracked
and amber replaced
black tourmaline.

You were soft as bones—
and that is a difficult thing to forget.

Not the End

Stay tuned for the next book in this
poetry trilogy: *I Used to Love You,*
by Chyana Marie Sage.

Chyana Marie Sage is nothing more and nothing less than a woman who dives into all aspects of life,

ebbing and flowing with the painful, the beautiful, the gut-wrenching, and heart-aching moments that find us.

There is beauty and lessons in all of it, and she welcomes it all with open arms.

 @softasbones

INDEX

Made in the USA
Coppell, TX
02 March 2021

51092750R00062